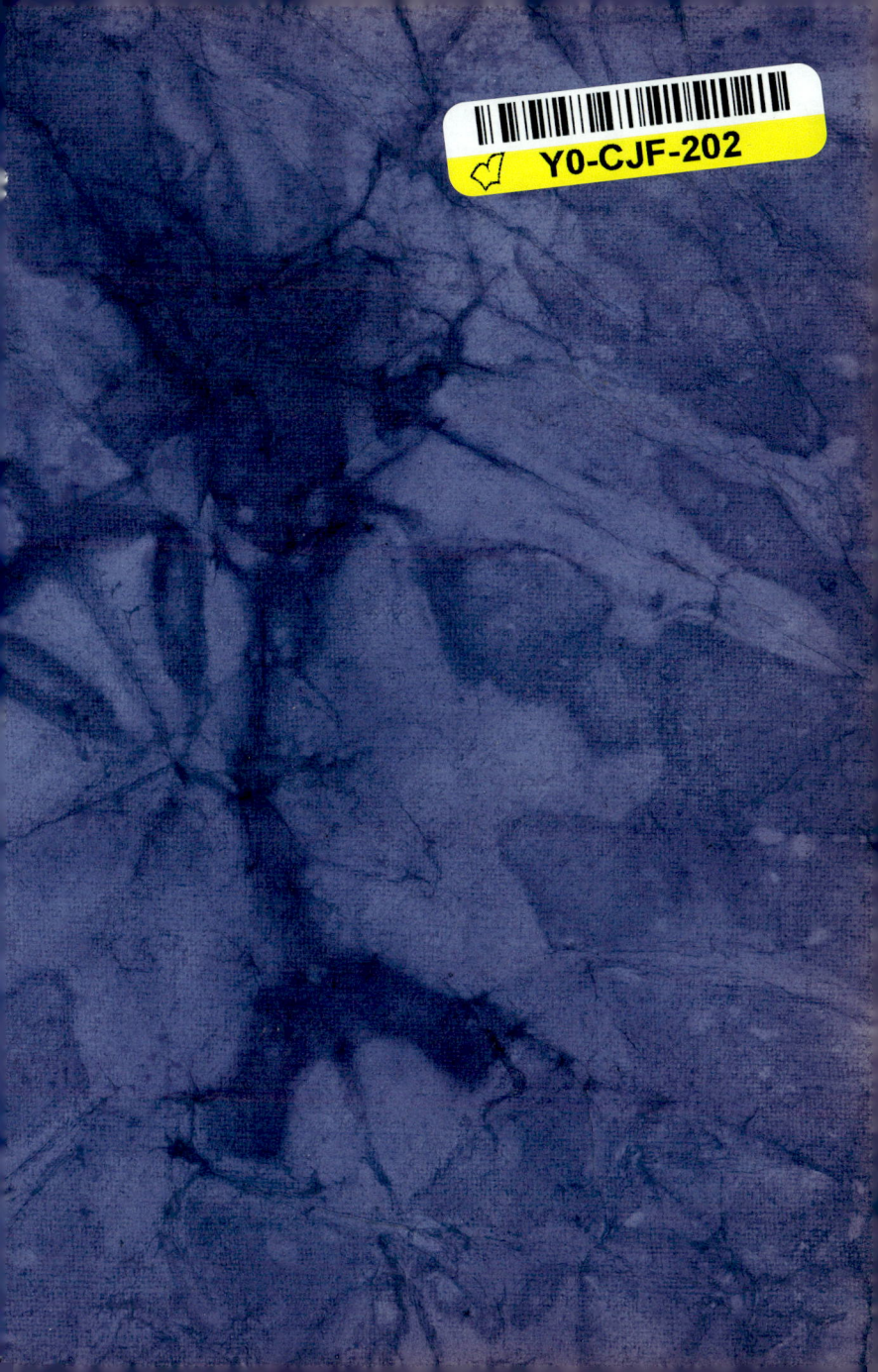

Take a Right at the Tank

&

Other Ways to Get Home

J. Nealin Parker

Take a Right at the Tank

&

Other Ways to Get Home

An Illustrated Photo-Journal of Liberia
With a Preface by
Ambassador Jacques Paul Klein

The Crumpled Press

New York, New York

Take a Right at the Tank & Other Ways to Get Home
© 2007 by J. Nealin Parker
Preface © 2007 by Jacques Paul Klein
All rights reserved

Portions of the text that previously appeared in the
Lexington News Gazette are reprinted with permission

Second Edition
ISBN: 978-0-9796969-0-9

Crumpled Press publications may be purchased for
education, enlightenment, trade, and tra-la-la

For further information please visit our website:

www.crumpledpress.org

Or write to:

The Crumpled Press
P.O. Box 20236
Greeley Square Station
New York, NY 10001-0006

Editors:

Alexander Bick
Nicholas Jahr
Jordan Kenneth McIntyre

For Rita and Junior

Contents

List of Plates
Preface, by Ambassador Jacques Paul Klein i

Take a Right at the Tank & Other Ways to Get Home

"It All"	1
Off to Visit	6
On the Ground	7
The Peacekeeper	8
Logos and Good Intentions	10
Understanding His People	13
Liberian Illness	15
Take a Right at the Tank	16
Sweat It Out Another Day	19
He Say I Don't Know Book	21
Elections Too Sweet	24
The Aid Worker's Equation	27
To Quit, Or Not To Quit	30
The Daily Commute	32

Hard Working White Woman	36
The Commander's Story	40
We Are What We've Been	46
It's Time	49
Fireflies and Fulfillment	53
I'm Back	55
The Election Commeth	57
Election Day	59
"It All"	62

List of Plates

1. Helen and Paye, orphans from the civil war, near Thinker's Village, Monrovia
2. Girls at a civic and voter education workshop in David-Semata, Lofa County
3. Liberians checking their names against the voter list during exhibition, Monrovia
4. Monrovia from a helicopter
5. A polling official assists voters on election day
6. The Monrovia-Gbarnga road
7. Roland, near Thinker's Village, Monrovia

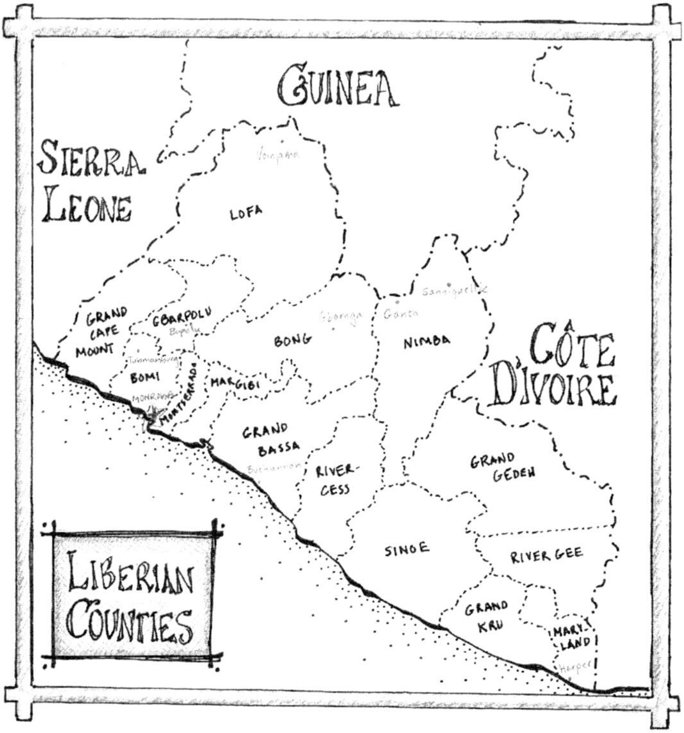
GUINEA
SIERRA LEONE
LOFA
GRAND CAPE MOUNT
GBARPOLU
BONG
NIMBA
BOMI
MARGIBI
MONTSERRADO
GRAND BASSA
RIVER-CESS
CÔTE D'IVOIRE
GRAND GEDEH
SINOE
RIVER GEE
GRAND KRU
MARYLAND
LIBERIAN COUNTIES

Preface

On July 26, 1847, Liberia declared its independence as the first African republic and proclaimed itself as the lone star—one of only two African states (the other being Ethiopia) that were never colonized. Thus, Liberia carries a heavy historical burden. Notwithstanding its recent problems, it has throughout its history markedly influenced African affairs and has exercised an international role far out of proportion to its size or its economic and demographic indicators. And also, sadly, from being a beacon of freedom in 1847 to a failed state in 2003, it is evident that Liberia has grown older but not necessarily wiser.

Today, Liberia stands at a critical juncture. Indeed, the challenges facing Liberia reflect, in many ways, the struggle of Africa as a whole. It is not by accident that Liberia finds itself at the epicenter of a highly volatile and unstable region which has recorded some of the most atrocious civil conflicts in recent history—conflicts which have brought unspeakable suffering to the peoples of the region. While Liberia remains the key to peace in West Africa, the region as a whole must contemplate which road will lead to lasting peace, genuine democracy, and sustainable development. Democracy is a sham and peace becomes elusive when development is not a concomitant part of the process.

As Special Representative of the Secretary-General, my mandate was to manage the largest United Nations (UN) peacekeeping operation in the world, UNMIL; oversee the implementation of the Comprehensive Peace Agreement (CPA) that was signed by the Liberian parties in Accra on August 18, 2003; and to coordinate the activities of the entire UN family in Liberia, which includes humanitarian and development agencies. Through the CPA, the former warring Liberian factions undertook to give peace a chance for the third time—first under Samuel Doe, then Charles Taylor, and now the three warring factions—within the timeframe of one generation.

As a result of the remarkable progress achieved so far in stabilizing Liberia and in implementing the mandate of UNMIL, presidential elections were held and, for the first time in a quarter century, Liberians were able to participate in a transparent, free and fair election. This election offered the Liberian people the opportunity to choose a leadership that hopefully will end the cycle of political violence, injustice, and endless human rights abuses that the population has endured for so long at the hands of cruel, hopelessly corrupt, and venal politicians.

The long suffering population yearns for nothing more than a safe and secure environment, good governance, and the opportunity to pick up the pieces of their shattered lives. Yet, in my more candid moments, I get apprehensive about whether Liberia's leaders have learned the lessons of why the country has three times fallen into decline and a political abyss, only to be rescued by large-scale international intervention.

I believe there are three critical lessons that the international community must learn as it works to secure Liberia's future. First, if the international community is able to provide the necessary support in reforming Liberia's security sector—through the creation of an armed forces premised on republican values, which represents the total spectrum of the ethnic character of Liberia and has a clear mandate to defend the integrity of the Liberian state—we will avoid one of the critical errors of past interventions in Liberia.

Second, if donors can commit fully to supporting the resources necessary for the more than 50,000 ex-combatants that still need to enter the reintegration and rehabilitation (RR) program, then we would have averted a grave mistake of past peace processes. Added to this, it is essential that Liberia's partners work with Liberians in ensuring that the skills and training acquired during the RR process are directly related to the needs of the post-conflict economy in order to assure the continued relevance of these skills for the regeneration of Liberia's economic base. This is particularly important because a whole generation of Liberians have been denied the opportunity to acquire both the technical and professional skills necessary to resuscitate the Liberian economy. The few who have managed to scale these hurdles are largely in the Diaspora.

Third, for real lasting and sustainable social and political change to take place in Liberia, international intervention should begin to focus on the development of strong ethical foundations which are underpinned by concern for the well-being of the individual and society. This goes to the heart of the fundamental dilemmas with which operators of peacekeeping operations are confronted. More often than not, the need to stabilize the theater and to neutralize armed elements works to the relative detriment of the development of proper values and ethics in the recipient society.

Having said all of this, there is a limit to what the international community can realistically deliver. Real change must come from within, and the international community can only be facilitators of that change by offering the necessary space and support.

Let me conclude by stressing that the mechanism we have put in place to ensure sustainable peace and security is also dependent on the cooperation and commitment of Liberians. We cannot force people to support the peace process or their newly elected government. We depend on their willingness to do so. In essence, Liberia's future hangs in the balance and only Liberians can tilt the scale in one direction or the other. The challenges are enormous: 50 percent of Liberians between the ages of one and 35 years have grown up without any idea of how a normal society operates. Yet, we cannot give way to despondency by underestimating the power of the will of a whole people. The choices for Liberians are clear.

As I indicated earlier, there is a critical need for a reorientation of the national spirit and concrete efforts by Liberians to elaborate a new vision for the future of their country. For all the good will of the international community, the fact is that international attention is often short and shifts like desert sand. Liberia's future cannot be built on sand—it must be built on hard work. There are few alternatives.

The struggle for Liberian renewal must first and foremost be centered on uniting its people and rebuilding the country. These are daunting challenges, but a patriotic call to national duty, requiring each and every Liberian to commit their individual and collective efforts to what is required, is now absolutely essential.

As to the spoilers and critics and all those who continue to undermine what is still very much a work in progress, I am reminded of an old proverb that states, "the dogs may continue to bark, but the caravan moves on."

And as a wise man once said, "it is not the critic who counts, or those who point out how the strong man stumbles, or where deeds could have been done better—ultimately, the credit belongs to those who are actually in the arena." To her credit, Nealin Parker has certainly been one of those who are very much in the arena.

Ambassador Jacques Paul Klein
Washington, DC
September 2006

Atlantic Ocean
United Nations Drive
Front
Broad
Carey
Benson St.
US Embassy
Mamba Point Hotel
UN Drive
apartments
EC Bilateral office
Fair Ground Rd.
Camp Johnson Rd
Mamba Point
Monrovia

Take a Right at the Tank

&

Other Ways to Get Home

"It All"

October 2004
Atlanta, Georgia
The Carter Center

I work feverishly in a windowless room, in a nondescript wooden cubicle, and in heels. I'm not sure which suits me less, but I don't care. I'm adrenaline-drunk from the surrounding efficiency and intellect of the policy makers and the former and foreign presidents. I am of the perky sort that wants to change the world and wants to be taken seriously when I say things like, "I want to change the world." To this end, I have been working at The Carter Center for over a year, but have just this week started working on Liberia. My first task is to create a briefing on the motley events of the newly initiated disarmament for a former ambassador who leads the Center's peace programs and will soon be traveling to Liberia.

I've read hundreds of articles about the country, the war, the peace process, and the events of the last 24 hours. I've distilled them into two pages of plane-reading for my boss. He is hopping the next flight over the ocean to Monrovia, Liberia, a city in the midst of post-war turmoil. This morning I've been on the phone with Jacques Klein, head of the UN peacekeeping mission in Liberia, trying to figure out if the country is falling back into mayhem or if the ex-combatants' demonstrations are merely routine post-civil war growing pains. Weeks ago, I didn't even know how to spell Klein's first name and most certainly didn't mean to be on the phone with him, but all that is now forgotten. He tells me the UN has barricaded itself in the compound. The city isn't safe. I relay this back to my boss. He is brave, head-strong, and off to make a difference anyway—and I, I wrote his briefing. God I'm marginal, but despite myself I finally feel like a part of it all; "It All" being a relatively fluid entity which has, for years, been the object of my curiosity and desire. I am torn. I want to call someone else brave and important and press him for more information; yet I equally want to call my mother and say something terribly efficient and informed to make her proud of me.

I have almost a compulsion for fixing things, or rather, for having the power to fix things. It can be explained by an infinite set of events in my life, I am sure. But if it did not begin when I first saw death, in Brazil, in 1988, on my father's research trip, then by that it was certainly emboldened:

Eight years old and sweating through my t-shirt and jean skirt, I share an ice cream cone with my sister who in all her appreciation is spreading more on her face and hands than she consumes. I am trying to prove the elevated rank that my extra four years afford me by making proper use of the napkin. I still have a child's relaxed belly. Next to us, my older brother, who at ten has started a growth spurt in his feet that will extend eventually throughout his entire body and even his hair, does not even need a napkin. He has a flat tummy that I associate with the vast experience his ten years have over my humble eight. And so I suck in my stomach as I wipe the ice cream off my own hands and my sister in her entirety. We only have two shirts each for this two-month trip, which we bring in the shower with us to wash and wear to dry. We shouldn't have gotten chocolate.

In my memory of the day, my parents are like technical assistants in the play of our world discovery, shifting lights, moving props, invisible, and yet orchestral and fundamental. Our drama now focuses on the ice cream that has dripped between my toes. I blame my little sister and entertain us in the wilting heat by sticking and un-sticking my toes together against the backdrop of the patterned sidewalks that lead to the dock. Unlike my toe tricks, the docks have gathered a crowd. My sticky skin looses its initial intrigue, and we follow the town's lead to the water's edge. I am, no doubt, holding my mother's hand. The memory is old enough that I trust it to be true without distinct details and I am not at all perplexed that the chocolate ice cream which so preoccupied me minutes before has vanished. I wriggle through the skirts and old dress pants, practicing my newly operational Portuguese. "*Desculpe-me*," I repeat with each hint of human contact. I want to counter any stereotypes they may harbor of *gringos* as loud and rude, but as a result of my limited vocabulary I merely overcompensate with copious apologies.

I squeeze through the last set of bodies and see a man tangled in rope, bobbing softly in the water, face down. His hair and dirty clothes are flowing gracefully with the gentle waves. The smell of rotting fish and trash and heat is overwhelming as I look up toward the Brazilian townspeople for direction and explanation. In the same dreamlike way my ice cream disappeared, I come into the knowledge that the man is, or was, the town drunk. He died the evening before, and, owing to the slow 'quick response' team at the hospital, he has yet to be picked up. Someone is—as he has been for hours—"on his way." Meanwhile, here on the edge of the dock, no one moves. The faces topping the bodies of the legs I prance through are impassive and, if anything, vaguely curious. It is my introduction to death, and I am appalled.

I search for my father, who speaks Portuguese, and on whom I can generally depend in times when something needs to be done. I don't know where he is, but he is not, as I believe he should be, jumping into the water, dragging the poor friendless degenerate onto the dock, and performing emergency mouth-to-mouth resuscitation. Looking at the corpse, I feel a piercing pain in my throat and chest, born from our personal connection: we are each someone's child. My eyes burn as I hold back tears. His clothes sway with a deceptively and disturbingly lively fluidity, and my empathy mixes with horror. He could still be alive, waiting for us! It should not be this way, but I feel powerless to change it.

We leave the man in the water. We leave the town. We leave the country. I grow up. I go to college. I move to Africa. I keep traveling, trying to understand, because I am serious when I say "I want to change the world," but when I say it, I'm still eight years old, and so I don't even take myself seriously. I've come to work for The Carter Center because, for all the controversy over his efficacy as a president, when Jimmy Carter says, "I want to change the world," people take him seriously. And so I now work on Liberia as if I owe it to a dead man, whom I can never repay, to fix it.

My boss gets on the flight later in the day, and I come in the next morning to read more articles and produce more briefs. I'm not as sure how important my distillation is today as the emergency departure has already taken place. I feel too far away again, and I know I am on the wrong end of that phone call with the UN in Liberia.

Nealin, David, Anson, and Laura
(Photograph by Phyllis Parker)

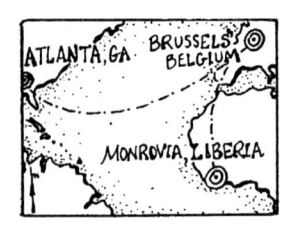

Off to Visit

April 2, 2005
Atlanta, Georgia
Flight to Brussels

"Happy Birthday, kiddo!" That's the phone call I mean to be making to my little sister right now. Instead I accidentally check my phone on the flight and have to borrow a fellow passenger's to call my roommate. "Coby, when you get this message—Jeff missed the plane. He left his ticket at the security check and didn't make it back in time. Anyway, I've got his carry-on luggage with me and I may have all his money, I don't know. I've tried to give the flight attendant 30 bucks to give to him for a cab, but she may not reach him before we take off. Sorry to do this, but can you pick him up? Thanks. See you back home in ten days!"

Jeff is moving to Liberia to be a Democracy Resource Officer for the next ten months, and I am off to visit briefly to help set up the main office. He'll be a few days later than anticipated, a fact in which I've now involved my section of the plane. Others are offering phones—as if with more phones I might remember more numbers. I have now delayed the flight by twenty minutes and am surprised by the kindness of my fellow passengers. This is not the romanticized departure of my boss six months earlier, but I imagine my sweat and high jinx are still more meaningful because they are all in the grand effort to "Build Democracy." The only way I can be part of "It All," really, is with some kind of absurd beginning.

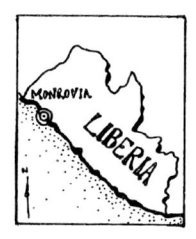

On the Ground

April 3, 2005
Monrovia, Liberia
Robertsfield International Airport

We have landed. The air is hot and somehow both wet and dusty. The English is fast and slurred. I stand by the side of my hotel's van while someone else deals with my paper work. I see Jacques Klein being ushered from the runway and into one of the hoard of white UN vehicles surrounding the airport, which equal in number those of various other international NGOs. A woman selling coke asks me if I want one. She'll take U.S. dollars, she says. I demure, but ask if she might teach me some of whatever languages she speaks. "EEL-ah-wak-bAY," I learn, means "what is your name?" in Kpelle, one of the 16 indigenous languages spoken in the country. "EEL-ah-wak-bAY?" I ask her. She giggles and says, "Mama."

What is your name?	Eel-ah-wak-bay?
My name is (Mama).	na-bah (Mama).
yes: oh-ay	no: bah
I am from America...	Aoh kūlah mohn??? wrm
I have one brother.	Hawah turnō.
I have one sister.	Dē-ah turnī.
I love your country.	Ē low-ay wehl-kah-ma.

The Peacekeepers

April 10, 2005
Monrovia, Liberia
Silver Beach

I squint my eyes and, like a camera coming into focus from a blinding whiteness, I see a man, or a boy, or something of both. He has light hair, a lanky body, and is not fully grown into himself. Khaki-green swimming trunks, loose and soaking, cling to his pale freckled legs. He looks sweet—as if his mom cried when he left, as if he cried too: for himself, for her, and for the sweet-young-thing he was leaving behind. Maybe he writes her love notes full of constrained emotion and implies more beneath the surface.

The waves crash hard, and he tries somewhat vainly to de-sand his inflated raft—the cheap, thin, air-mattress kind that are long and rectangular like the one I used to take to the city pool. He is performing awkwardly. As he cleans, he must let go of his raft with his left hand to grab his gun and keep it from shifting down his back. He is a UN peacekeeper. He looks vulnerable and idiosyncratically powerful, as many foreign people here seem—here to fix a problem in Liberia, dependent on Liberians to know how to tie his own shoes. Awkward. Powerful. Naked, save wet swimming trunks. Gun slung across his shoulder.

Behind him, a row of his Swedish cohorts tan on army-issued green lawn chairs that sit no more than eight inches off the sand. Just enough space for a cloth and their guns underneath.

UN Peacekeepers at Silver Beach

Logos and Good Intentions

April 18, 2005
Monrovia, Liberia
Jack's Bar and Grill

I've managed to find reasons for The Carter Center to keep me in Monrovia. I've told them I will be the "Democracy Resource Coordinator and Security Officer," a management position that did not previously exist, but whose description includes training six expatriate staff from Africa and Europe and helping them deploy to three new offices in the interior of the country. There they will provide technical assistance for political parties, organize voter education, and train domestic observers for the election. To ensure that my role is more essential here than in Atlanta, I offer to design their deployment plan and collect their reports. I collaborate with a logistics consultant to establish their offices, then create and enforce security policies, as well as any number of other things that continue to arise as the new project finds its feet. The Carter Center extends my stay in week-long intervals, and I retain the high-impact schedule of the 16-hour workday because it's all so temporary. Three times a week I could be on Liberia's only Europe-bound flight, on my way back home. Three times a week I find myself ignoring the flight and instead staying another night in the best hotel in the country.

Across the street from the hotel is a colorful, if seedy, beach bar that plays a combination of country music and Afro-Caribbean polka. A smorgasbord of security, service, government, and nongovernmental institutions leave their logos lying around on their jackets, hats, brief cases, and notebooks in the familiar forms of security tags, t-shirts, and business cards. People at times refer to each other as their respective institutions saying, "That's EU," or they distinguish further by usefulness, adding, "She's UN—and knows people." It's part strategy, part fear, and part laziness that clusters us all in places like this bar. Strategy: Here you can get information over a drink you'd never manage in a business meeting. Fear: We feel safe and comfortable with other aid workers who, just like us, made the long trek to this post-conflict paradise. Laziness: We don't have to work to communicate. In this bar, we all speak "aid worker."

Perhaps I am being too harsh. This afternoon, coming back into town from the beach, I watched a man chase a woman through a field. He ran with the base of a chair in his hand and twice tried to throw at her. She disappeared behind a wall as he picked up bottles and stones and hurled them at her before he, too, disappeared. Pewee, a Liberian staff member, Associated Press photographer, and friend, slowed the car to a crawl and said he wished he'd had his camera. I stayed in the car. Watched. Thought of what to do. Thought of going back. Thought of telling the UN policeman down the street. But for all my consideration, in the end, I rode home silently.

So I think myself a coward. When Pewee explains that the UN police have no power of arrest and will instead call the local police—who have no transportation, and in any case are especially unsuccessful with domestic abuse cases, because women fear accusing their fathers and husbands—I become impressed with the monumental excess of aid infrastructure that is invested in Liberia, yet doesn't seem to diminish any of the problems. Disheartening, really: all these logos, misguided programs, good intentions and lack of mandate.

MONROVIA, LIBERIA . MAMBA POINT.

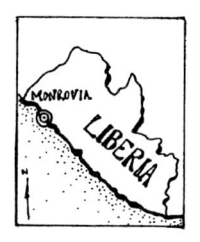

Understanding His People

April 19, 2005
Monrovia, Liberia
Civic Education Training

Muhammad, a man from "Concerned Mandingo Citizens of Liberia," sits in front of me at a voter and civic education training. The Mandingo are one of the many ethnic groups in Liberia, like Bassa and Kissi. They live predominantly in the north of the country, but also in neighboring Guinea. Having a modern border drawn through their lands has repeatedly caused their nationality to be called into question—"Are they really Liberian?" I've heard people ask.

The man is wearing a strikingly crisp brown suit. It is almost the same color as his skin and exactly the same color as the UPS uniforms in the States. Over one shoulder he carries a black bag with the words "Mary Kay" neatly silk-screened in gold on the lower right hand corner. He is tall, strong, and thick. He asks me if we can be friends and his majestic stature softens to sweetness. He tells me his people have been through much. . . too much. He wants to "make it better" in the future. He says all this with an inquiring smile. Gentle anticipation. Hopeful connection and understanding. I sit behind him and wonder at the healed gash behind his left ear. His skull dips in and the re-grown skin puffs out in over-compensation, noticeably bare despite his short hair. I wonder if I will know what has happened to his skull, what happened to him, what, exactly, happened to his people.

N
Sierra Leone
Guinea
Kissi
Mende
Gbandi
Mandingo
Loma
Gola
Kpelle
Mende
Bele
Vai
Gola
Kpelle
Mandingo
Mano
Dei
Bassa
Gio
Côte D'Ivoire
Kru
Bassa
Krahn
Sapo
Grebo
Kru
16 Liberian Ethnicities

Liberian Illness

April 20, 2005
Monrovia, Liberia
The Office

Of the six Carter Center staff deployed to the interior, one is hospitalized, and one is either ill or so depressed that she may need to be brought back to Monrovia. Their partners are almost fully preoccupied with their care. Furthermore, our logistics guru thinks he may have malaria; one of our local staff has typhoid and malaria; and Pewee's malaria has flared to a +2. I would have been hospitalized with a +1 because I have no resistance, but Pewee, as with most Liberians, is in a perpetual malarial state and +1 for him apparently is simple discomfort.

The amount of illness people in this country bear is, by all rights, unbearable. To the Liberian staff, however, it seems so standard as to be unworthy of note. I only discovered their illnesses when I spent hours on the phone with an international medical insurance group after a deployed staff member's heart stopped. As he'd failed to report any worrying signs previously, the next day I marched in and, as part of our program's Security Plan, demanded to know every single abnormal bodily function anyone in the room had faced in the last six weeks. "Anyone who is even the least bit sick needs to tell me now!" Almost every Liberian hand in the room tentatively straggled upward—typhoid, malaria, the fever. And so, with this health report we usher in the Registration Period.

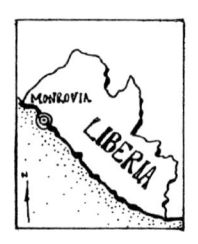

Take a Right at the Tank

Early May 2005
Monrovia, Liberia
My House

I live on a dirt road with no name in the middle of downtown Monrovia. My house is large, open, and sparsely furnished in wicker. I invite friends over to celebrate the marking of permanence that comes from moving out of a hotel.

"Take UN Drive. Take a right at the tank that guards Chairman Bryant's house. Then take your first left at that Egyptian restaurant that I think is a brothel. Mine's the last house before the bend in the path, between the compounds of *Medecins Sans Frontiers* (MSF) Belgium and MSF France." It may be the only time in my life that directions to my house will employ a tank as a useful landmark. There is a disturbing humor in giving these directions, which I relish.

A few friends arrive and we sit on the back porch until evening, then move inside when the air is cooler and the generator is turned on. It is a reassuringly uneventful evening. The next morning I wake to begin the harried pace of work anew. My bedroom is the only room without air conditioning, but what it lacks in climate control, it makes up for in view. Beyond the wall of sliding glass windows, screens, and steel grates in front of me, there are three palm trees, a water tower, a few Italian clay roofs that shelter squatters in blown-out buildings, and beyond all this, the ocean stretching toward the Equator, some five degrees to the south.

To my left, there is something of an African slum-turned-medieval-village. Cement houses are formed over and into a rock face. Boulders shape stairways. Flattened spaces become community centers.

My neighbors across the razor wire have started showering outside, as they do about two times a week around this time of morning. Sometimes, when it rains, they take soap and a bucket and stand in the rain, and it makes me laugh to think that I pull my curtains to change clothes.

When first I arrived, Rita, the house cleaner, and Barcon, the cook, stood by the doorway in a line to welcome me. I hugged them to say "hello." I didn't know how self aware my greeting was; if I was trying to overcome years of classism by diminishing the formality; or if that is just the way we like to say "hello" in small town Virginia. In any case, it was the first in a series of actions that indicated to both of them that I did not know how to run a household. Rita and Barcon trained me to ask for dinner, leave money to go shopping, and lock my valuables. They now make my bed, heat a pot of water for my morning bath, find my vagrant socks, iron out the mold blooming on everything I own, turn down my collar as I run out of the house, and chase me down with my briefcase and an extra bottle of water when I forget—which is often.

I live a bizarre and incongruous life only possible in the developing world. I have electricity only certain hours and I bathe out of a bucket. My phone malfunctions daily. There is no internet when it rains, and in a few months I won't be able to walk down the street on account of the flooding. On the other hand, I don't wash my own dishes, take out my trash, sweep my floor, or drive myself. Five people are paid to stand at my door and open it when I come home. Another ten guard my office door. One man is paid to turn the generator on and off, another to rake the trash. Both stay by the house all day in case there is an immediate need for their services—the former sleeps by the generator all night as well. It is all the service you could want if you wanted it at all, but the inequality is too blatantly unjustified to allow me to delight in the comfort.

As I look back from my neighbors' homes to the papers spread over my bed, I am making sleepy efforts to review the National Elections Commissions (NEC) weekly updates on the registration process. Until now, the NEC needed only to convince its own staff to participate in preparations, but with the registration, all of Liberia's estimated 1.5 million eligible voters must be coaxed into taking part. I say "estimated" because there has been no census since 1984. This was a necessary decision to keep the election timetable, but one that forced the NEC to almost blindly plan its registration centers using outdated old maps or inaccurate new maps that mark cities which have been wiped out and, in any case, take no account of many camps for internally displaced persons and refugees. It is not just that we must estimate the population at three million, and once again estimate that half this number are eligible voters. We must also find these people and register them. I envision the process as something like opening a new restaurant: we have printed the menus and hired the waiters, and now we just need the country to bite.

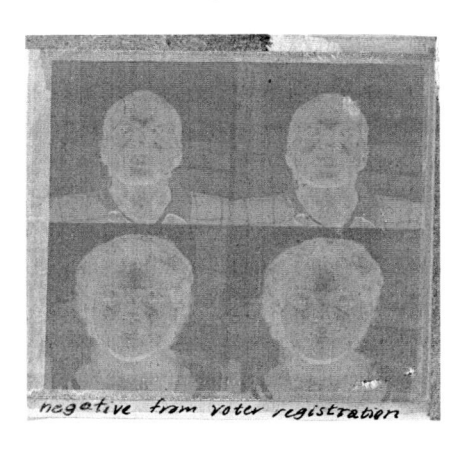

negative from voter registration

Sweat it Out Another Day

May 7, 2005
Monrovia, Liberia
Medicins Sans Frontiers Clinic

Each of the rooms harbors a distinct pungency, thick with the aromatic manifestation of sick, sweaty humans. Each wooden cot supports a limp black body puddled in the middle. Mismatched squares of fabric, sewn together and hung on plastic piping, divide one sickness from another. But the smells, the smells weave around the divide and meet each other to combine into something rich and sweet and acridly alive.

Outside in the hall, all ages of the seemingly forsaken line the wall with hollow stares, sunken eyes, and limp, bony appendages. Everywhere is stoicism. Healthy, fat nurses in scrubs stand out starkly. They convey comforting smiles and even more comforting physiques.

I have a viral infection. I have dutifully given my blood sample (rather effortlessly laying on one of the cots) and my stool sample (rather awkwardly in a plumbing-less bathroom, using a stick and a tea cup). I will go home and sweat it out like everyone else. Only I am not like everyone else. I have the distinct sense that I'm immortal, and there is absolutely no question that I will live to sweat it out another day. The immortality of the foreigner, the wealthy, the entitled, stands out as sharply as the elbows and knees of my fellow patients. Growing up, my mother used to remind me that my youth did not make me immortal. She never told me whether or not money did.

I want so much to understand Liberian lives, but I am not willing to give up my everlasting existence and to languish here. And so I allow myself to be bumped to the front of the line and then I allow myself to acquire the best medicine money can buy. I'll return home with near death stories, maybe, but I will certainly return home.

The staff in front of my office
(Photograph by Pewee Flomoku)

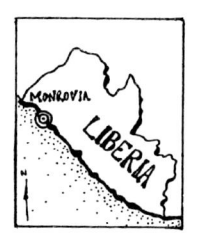

He Say I Don't Know Book

Mid-May 2005
Monrovia, Liberia
My House

At my new house, the security guards can hardly stare at anything else. I am entertained by their feigned professional patrolling of our grounds—excuses to look longingly indoors at the woman ironing my clothes. If they are lucky or cunning, they will have managed to run out of water and will have a legitimate reason to lean in the door and engage her in conversation. They will even have a second in which to slip a suggestive wink as they thank her, all under the watchful eye of the one part patriarchal, two parts grandfatherly Bassa cook, Barcon. His strict rules of the house neither allow the guards further entry, nor allow Rita, the object of their fascination, enough leeway to find herself in a compromising position.

Rita is twenty-four, tall, and what she calls, "supa-sleen," by which she means a waist the size of one of my thighs with matching spaghetti thin neck, arms, and legs. All these slender and delicate appendages articulate on an anything but super-slim set of hips. The combination is terribly dramatic and attractive to just about anyone who sees her, a fact that is regularly confirmed by jealous expatriate women and the intoxicated stares of my helplessly taken guards. I want to say she looks 17 or 18, either because of the baby t-shirts and mini-skirts she wears or because I always manage to underbid the age of Liberians, but her poise and self-confidence indicate otherwise.

Rita has come in crying. She and her boyfriend have "made confusion." She can barely form the words. She says quietly in a thick Liberian accent, "He say I don't know book," and adds that it was in public, around their friends. This is one insult she cannot bear. It is true. She cannot read—which only makes it worse.

She needs to justify her illiteracy to me, though I require no such justification. Some time during the war, around 1993, a 12-year-old Rita, shy and every bit as lanky as she is today, would not leave her house for fear of the gunfire. Her mother did not know what to do with her diffidence, so when a Lebanese woman approached and offered to take the meek and timid child away from the fighting and put her in school in Lebanon, she acquiesced. Bewildered and shell-shocked, Rita flew with the woman to Lebanon and was handed over to a new family immediately upon landing. This new family, self-righteous for having saved a war-damaged child, gave Rita a mat to sleep on in the kitchen, beatings, and no salary. They barred any communication with her family, and, after her first attempt to escape, locked her in the house. On her second attempt—ten years after arriving in Lebanon—Rita finally escaped to the Liberian Embassy and, despite a hitch in her paperwork (she never had any), was flown back to her home country. She no longer spoke her native language, Mano, and could not talk with her mother when they were finally reunited. She holds no visible anger towards this family, but says simply, "Some people know how to keep people, some do not." I start to see something very enlightened in Rita.

Later, Rita and I begin lunchtime reading classes. She and her boyfriend make up. I secretly continue to dislike him even as I understand the complications involved in the quiet recesses of our hearts. Were I able to disentangle love, the Liberian elections would be simple.

Rita

Elections Too Sweet

May 14, 2005
Harper, Liberia
The Tea Shop

Harper is a well-loved, well-worn city just west of the border with Ivory Coast. During the rainy season, the road washes out and it becomes inaccessible by road from Monrovia. Even during the dry season it is a two-day trip in a sturdy truck with a winch to pull you through stretches where the dirt and gravel roads all but disappear into the surrounding foliage. I have taken an hour-long UN flight to get here. I am to visit our Democracy Resource Officers who cover the southern section of the country. Former Liberian President, William Tubman, comes from this beach area. He too woke up to fat rain drops punctuating the hum of high pitched insects, the three-tiered frog conversation, the delicate trickle of water searching for the lowest proximal puddle, the indistinguishable voices of the house staff as they carry buckets of water for the day's activities, and children laughing in the trees, picking barely ripened mangoes—or plums, as they're called in Liberia.

I am staying down the street from the UN airstrip—a flattened stretch of clay and a tent with barbed wire surrounding it. If you continue past the house where I stay, down Airstrip Road, there is a commercial center. After a few non-descript huts and just before the unassumingly named "Trying to Try Entertainment Center," there stands "The Tea Shop." Three benches rise up to a high counter along three sides of the hut. Inside there is one bag of oats, one tin of lard, four jars each of Ovaltine, sweetened condensed milk, and coffee, one box of Lipton's tea bags, a large bag of sugar divided into tens of little bags which may be bought individually, one gas stove, two pots, one pan, a tin of salt and pepper, and three sturdy employees—all of whom look under the age of twenty five. One, a warm featured woman named Etna, wears a Green Day shirt with a Simpsons-esque cartoon on the front. She does not revel in the punk-rock music of Green Day, I imagine, but has acquired the article as a cast off of a cast away through the Red Cross. Another, a strong decent-looking boy, wears a shirt that states, with one word on top of the other and the first letter of each in red highlighting, "So Happy I've Turned 40!" The third in the shop is younger—probably 14, but he looks about nine. Here one has the option of having beverages "sweet small small" or "too sweet." I order "Ovaltine too sweet" and watch a fourth of my cup fill with sweetened condensed milk.

When it rains, which is everyday at this time of year, women and children sit on the front bench dangling their feet under the corrugated tin awning. The Tea Shop doesn't seem to keep hours as such. It opens when there are people to drink tea; it closes when there are none. The Tea Shop, a particularly Liberian entity, is the epicenter of political discourse in each town and borough. I wish I could pour the easy and full knowledge that my servers have of Liberian existence into my brain as easily as they pour sweetener into my ovaltine. It is my first time leaving the capital, and I am now beginning to realize how very little I know.

View from the Masonic Temple, Harper
(Photograph by Alexander Bick)

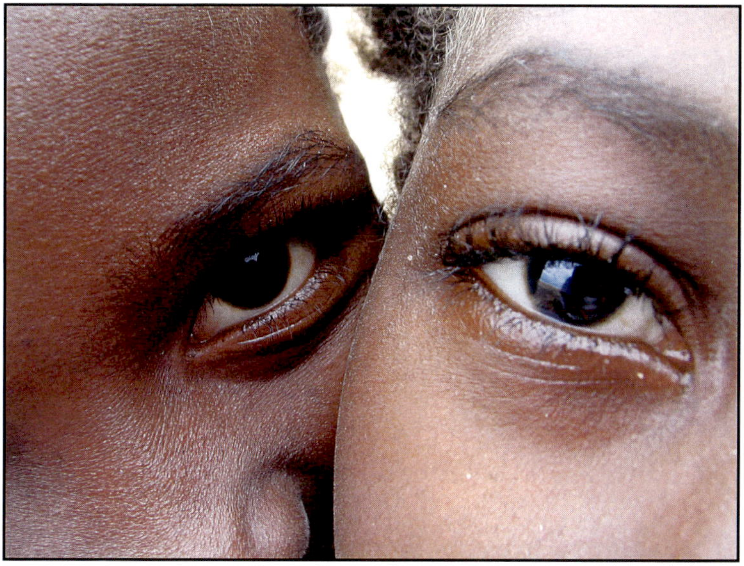

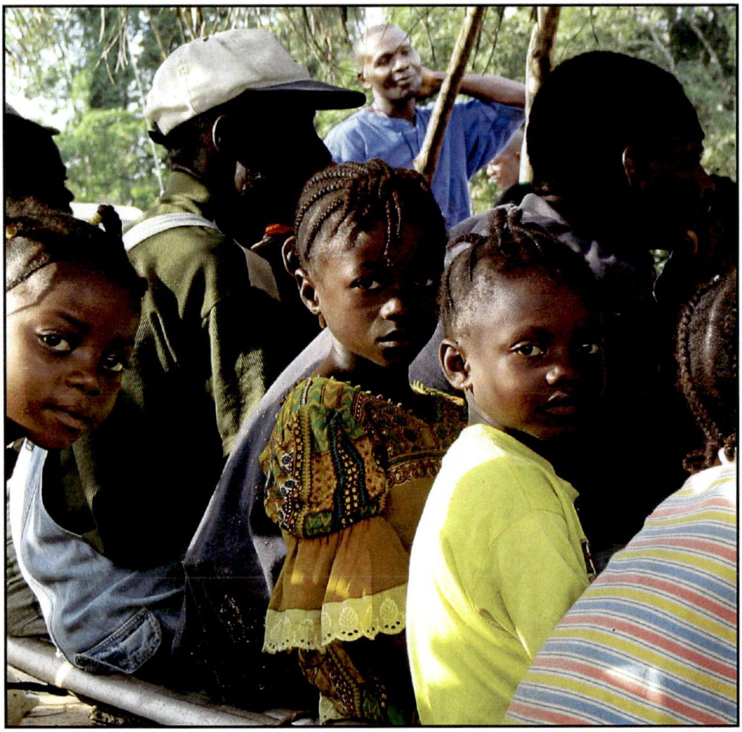

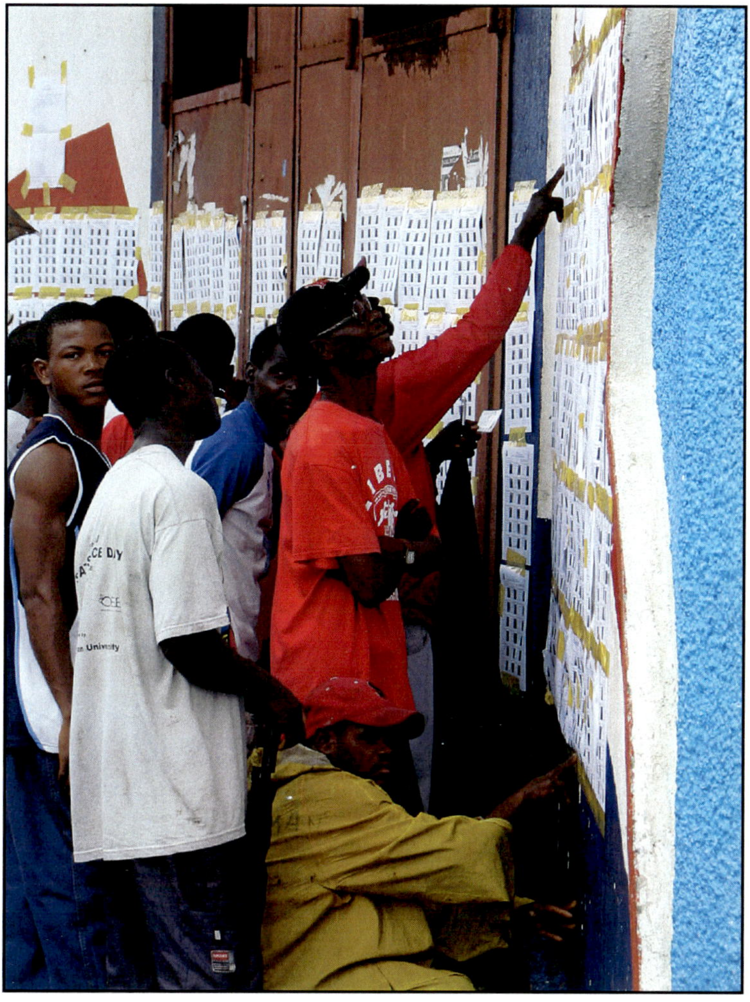

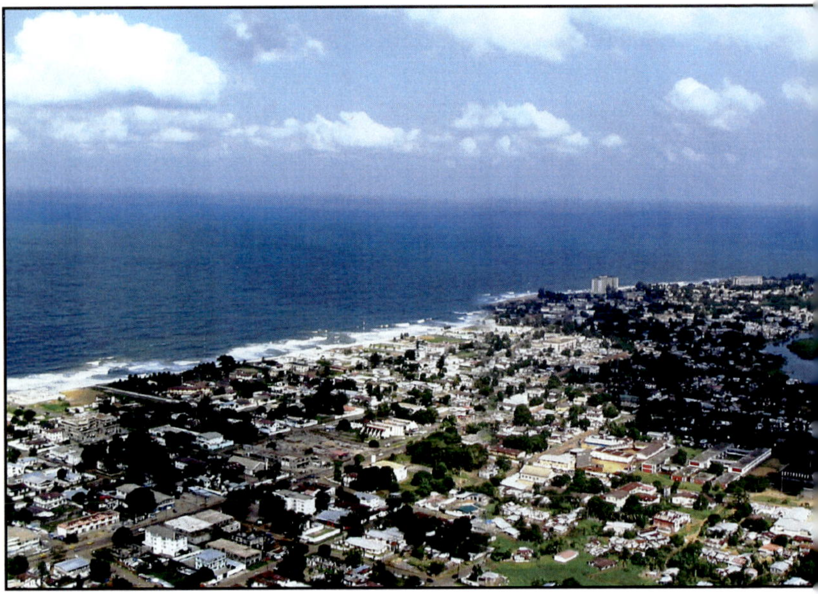

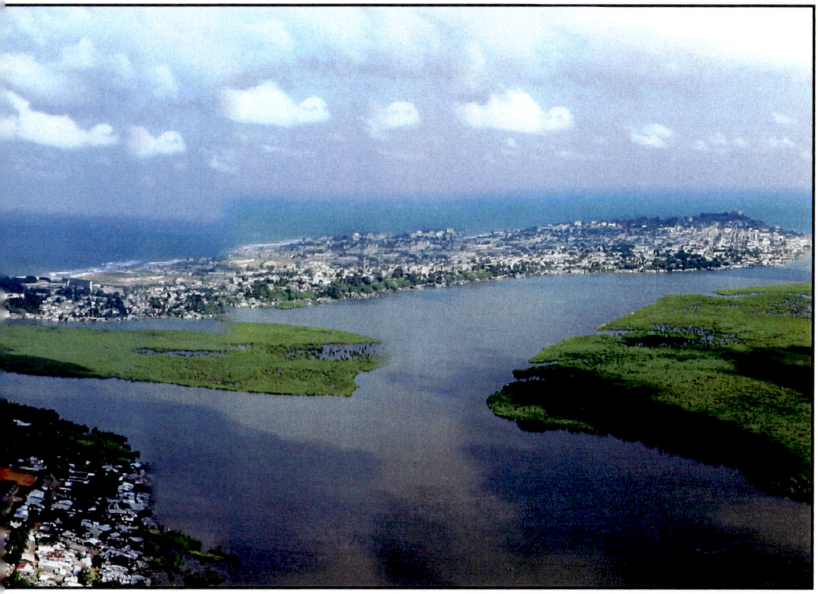

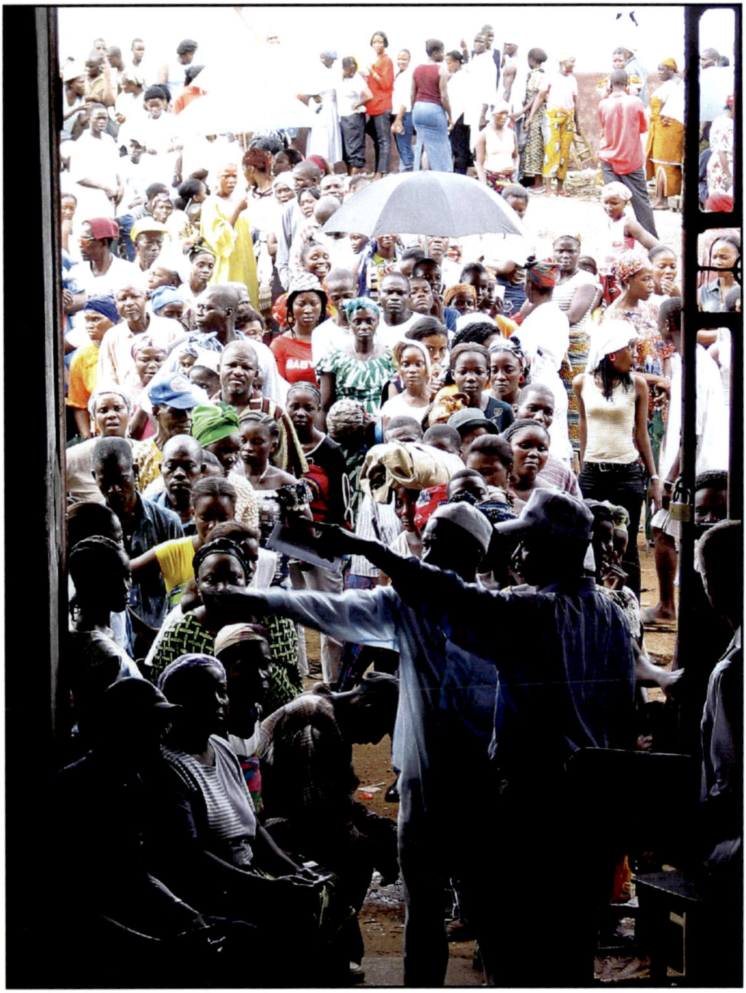

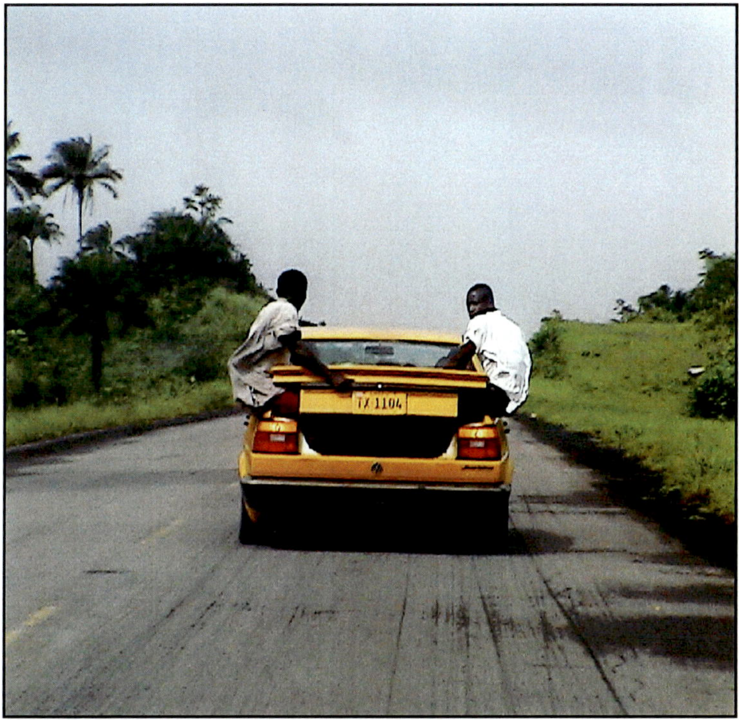
TX 1104

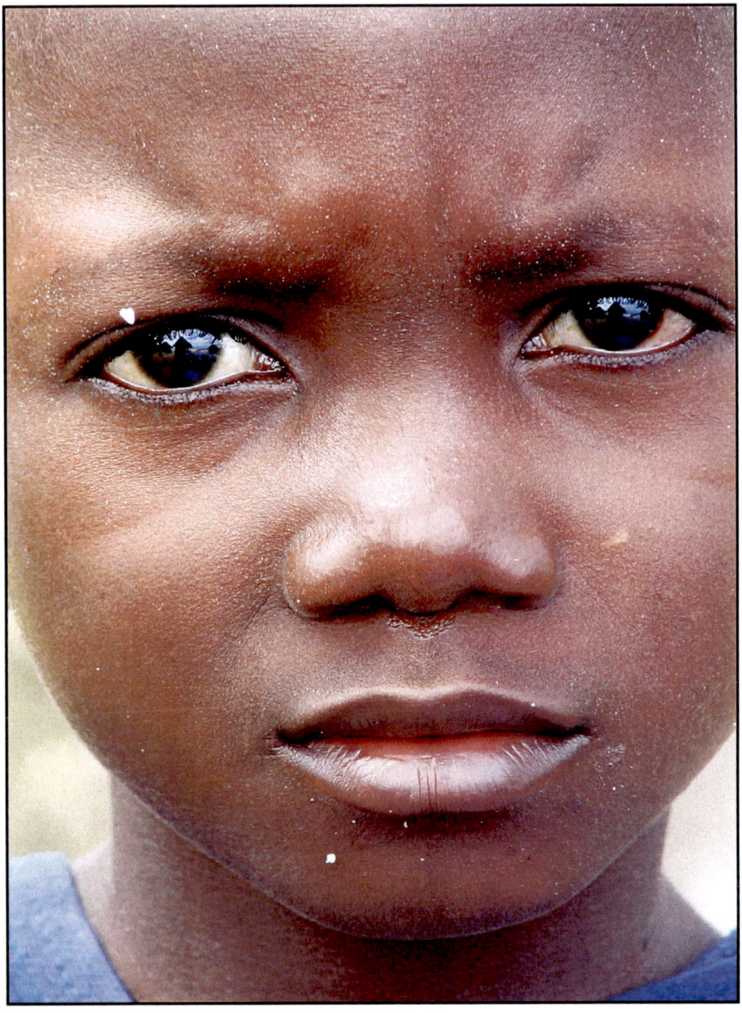

The Aid Worker's Equation

May 15, 2005
Harper, Liberia
European Commission Elections House

Last night I slept on a low wooden bed made by an ex-combatant on blue and white tie-dyed sheets and a thin foam mattress. The only decoration in my room is a dramatically colored African-print curtain covering one window directly above my bed. The house has no electricity and no running water. I wash in a bathtub by scooping water from a bucket into a cup and pouring it over me. I am tired and all parts of me are covered in a film of sticky so that I can't even be bothered to take off my clothing as I lie on the bed in the intermittent breeze.

We had dinner on the fourth floor of an aid-worker's office and residence overlooking the lake and the ocean beyond. A now defunct lighthouse marks the final tip of land, beyond which Liberian men with sleek muscles skillfully maneuver dugout canoes through soft waves.

Almost all of us are new to Liberia. We banter and postulate plausible futures. I have no idea whether anyone's assertions are correct, so I become quiet and am informed that perhaps the country will collapse because the demobilization process has run out of money. Because the government corruption is so pervasive there will be no infrastructural development. Because people will remain dissatisfied and they are not tired of fighting, as are people in Mozambique. Because, when Guinea's ailing President dies, instability there will spill over into northern Liberian cities. Because neighboring Cote d'Ivoire is equally volatile, and a conflict in either would send huge numbers of refugees across the border and further destabilize the region. Because former president and warlord, Charles Taylor, is supporting phantom groups we call political parties, who will invite him back after the election. Because Americo-Liberian parties, should they take over, will suck the life and progress out of any efforts in the counties. Because the Lebanese are pulling strings, promising funds. Because of vote-buying. Because of the Monrovia-interior divide. Because the international community is pulling funding and nobody really cares anyway. Because the country does not care about promises of democracy. Because the voting population neither understands the purpose of registration, nor trusts the motives of the NEC. Because the U.S. will determine the next president anyway. Because the National Transitional Legislative Assembly has proposed and passed a bill to postpone elections until December. All these assessments seem as patently bold as they are infuriatingly uninformed.

It is my first time leaving the capital, and I am just beginning to realize how little everyone else knows.

Even what must pass, relatively speaking, for optimism (perhaps more sympathy for the country, really) is often couched in condescension. "Ah, but the people deserve better, are so friendly, have been through so much." "The country is beautiful; has been beautiful." "There are so many international resources being put here; not enough, mind you, but still, they should be able to do something with it."

Against this backdrop, we may discuss our work in straightforward proposal terms: "We employ 600 ex-combatants at one dollar a day." "We operate a free clinic." Or in less straightforward, more nebulous terms: "We are supporting education efforts." "We work in sustainable development." Or even in irrelevant terms: "We're on an EU grant." "We work in 42 countries around the world." All of this emphasizing the divide between the donors and the country for which we must act as a bridge. We may tout some successes or discuss our failures in terms of what "went wrong," but more often than not it is what someone else did wrong: the "system," the Liberian work ethic, etc.

And so we internationals have a conversational formula that helps us to preserve our own sanity:

- A) The problems are big, too big, and too many
- + B) I have sympathy, but don't forget how big the problems are, and that, ultimately, it is neither my responsibility nor under my control
- + C) Here is what I do, because despite A + B, I care.

- D) . . . equals what?. . .
- D) Give me a break. I am trying. (Said desperately and compellingly)
- D) It's pretty crazy, isn't it? (Said neutrally, with some excitement, like one has just discovered a fun fact)
- D) Hell of a life. Hell of a world. (Said neutrally, with eyes down cast, head shaking, sort of grandfatherly and nostalgic)
- D) My failure to effect meaningful change that alters any of the problems I have highlighted does not cause a perpetual identity crisis. (Not said... Thought)

And herein lies the spectrum of detachment. Is Liberia mine to care for and to care about, or not? And if it is not mine, how did I in good conscience come here? And if it is mine, how do I in good conscience continue?

To Quit, Or Not To Quit

May 29, 2005
Monrovia, Liberia
The Office

It is my last day of work in Liberia. I extended as long as I could, and I'm not supposed to be here anymore—at least not on the grant that funds my project. A long bureaucratic process has determined that I must return to Atlanta if I want to remain employed. We are celebrating the success of the registration process. Approximately 1.3 million Liberians decided it was worth the walk—which for some meant a two-day journey when all was said and done—and this means I can leave feeling as though I am contributing to something the country cares about.

It's a notable day for other reasons, though. One of our security guards, Emmanuel Sieh, had a daughter on May 24, 2005. Emmanuel has a young, wide-eyed smile and a playful appreciation for morning greetings. He wanted me to learn his name and quizzed me every time I entered the gate until I did. Although our greetings as I enter in the morning and depart in the evening are the extent of our social interaction, he has named his daughter "Nealin Siehnyeno Sieh." I cried when he told me this morning, and he called his wife to have her come in to meet me. I gave her my picture, a lucky penny, forty dollars (his month's salary), and my folks' telephone number in the U.S. I took pictures. I am told Nealin laughs sometimes, even though she is only a week old. I joke that we have the same eyes.

I wonder if Liberians will ever know how to pronounce "Nealin," and imagine her at five, and ten, and twenty, and fifty, explaining to her peers, "no, not LEEna, NEAlin." I feel that I must grow up and into my position as namesake. I'm the only Nealin I've ever known. Now there's a second. And in my unabashedly romanticized notion of existence, I feel myself permanently a part of Africa.

I decide to quit my job and stay.

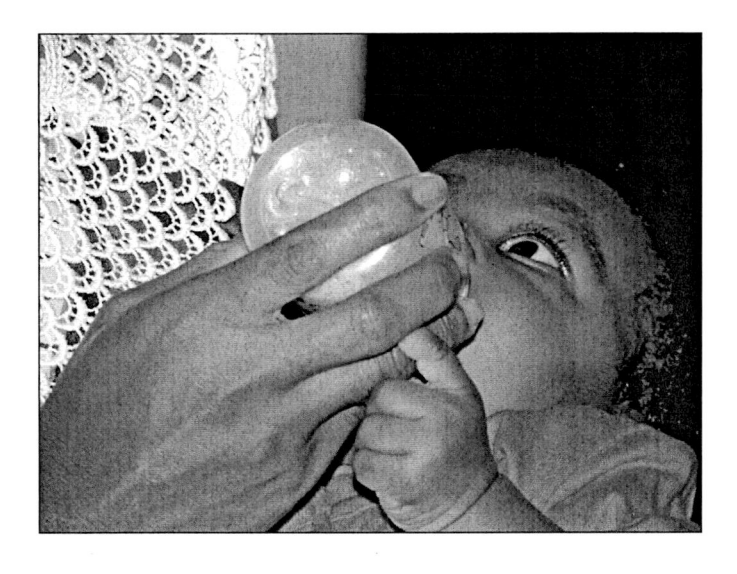

Nealin Siehnyeno Sieh

The Daily Commute

June 7, 2005
Monrovia, Liberia
UN Helicopter

Again I am on a UN helicopter, writing during its customary 15-minute shaking period as it hovers inches above the ground. Heat from the engine wafts through the portal windows. The two Liberians across from me in the helicopter are praying, vehemently. All our bags are piled in a three-foot-high line the length of the helicopter. Two benches with seatbelts run down the sides. The Russian crew has already indicated the three exits in thick, syrupy accents. In comforting constancy, we will lift off toward the ocean and swing around over Bushrod Island.

After five minutes in the air, the small hills with burr-like palm trees will unfold, expanding into the unidentifiable blue distance. Another five minutes and we'll fly over commanding impassable muddy rivers, water barreling quickly over rocks despite the meander more characteristic of an old river.

Soon we'll land on the red clay of Tubmanburg after passing the palm tree swamp and the plateau that I've heard is a diamond mine active before the imposition of UN sanctions. During our ten-minute stopover, gracious Pakistani soldiers will shuffle down with a tray of lemonade and a package of cookies. We will mill about. Men will walk to the edge of the landing pad and relieve themselves. We rarely pick anyone up from Tubmanburg, but always soldiers come to meet us. They strut with confident authority.

It is not until our second leg that we'll pass over the larger hills, typical of northern Liberia, and I will think it must be like living in broccoli, a never ending ocean of broccoli with an occasional river of palm trees. The magnitude of the trees is only obvious by comparison to the smallness of the huts they shade.

If it is wet outside, we'll close our little circular portal windows and the thick smell of warm, un-bathed bodies will fill the compartment. The pungency will make us drowsy. We will lean over our knees or back onto the metal casing, our heads bumping lightly in unison, challenging the validity of chaos theory as we shake and roll under the clouds and try to sleep the smells and the airsickness away.

But, if it is neither raining nor crowded, I will lie across three or four seats with my head propped on my emergency kit, the wind blowing across my face, watching the powerful African rainforest flowing beneath me. I will try not to take more pictures. I will fail.

I will smile quickly at other passengers before we each turn back to the scenery outside our metal box. These punctuating acknowledgements of each other's presence are the extent to which we can relate before conversation is made impossible by the blare of the motor and propeller.

I will know I am flying north if I cannot have conversation with the Pakistani soldiers, East if I cannot speak with Bangladeshis, and South if it is the Senegalese I cannot hear—each nationality silently flying to his respective peacekeeping borough. When we land back in Monrovia, we'll silently pack our things

Nealin looking out the UN helicopter window
(Photograph by Carmina Sanchis-Ruescas)

into our under-20 kg bags, or pull them from under the rope netting at our feet. Accustomed to our own silence, or maybe awkward because of how little we've interacted in the several hours we've spent with each other, we slide out, bumble out, shuffle out, without conversation.

Today it is the two Liberians reestablishing their relationship with God and several Pakistani's with whom I travel. We are flying north to a county NEC office.

Over the weekend after I quit my job I got lucky. Another democracy-building organization needed someone to help finish these county offices. I commute on a helicopter from one county seat to another every day now, acting as a building contractor, a task for which I am equipped only by my volunteer work with Habitat for Humanity and some odd jobs I did in college to make extra money.

Peacekeeper and Liberian onlookers at the helipad

Hard Working White Woman

June 15, 2005
Gbarnga, Liberia
The NEC Office

The helicopter touches down and its passengers pour out unsteadily into the sun. I hitch a ride from the helicopter-landing field to the building site and ask the group of men standing outside which one is the foreman.

The foreman is tall with kind eyes and an easy smile that exposes a gap between his front teeth. He has paint all over his body. We walk from room to unfinished room discussing all that needs doing. We check a few boxes on my form indicating that an item has been finished and write lengthy comments about those items that require more labor. I hand him our worksheet, for which he thanks me. This is his building, not mine, so I walk outside to leave him to work. He has promised it will all be finished on time (in three hours, when the contractor is to arrive).

My job today is to be present for the handover of the keys of the two Bong County NEC Offices. They were supposed to have been completed prior—much prior—to my arrival.

Ten minutes pass with no action. I ask again.

"You've got seven workers and four of them have been sitting and watching me for the last ten minutes," I stammer. He laughs—not at me, I think, but I'm not laughing, so not with me either. "You've got three hours until handover." Same laugh.

I am aware of my cultural boundaries. I am white and thus

expected to be (or at least act like) the "bo-lay," a Liberian English form of the unappealing title, "boss-lady," which to me conjures up images of Liberia's connections to slavery. As much as I might want to shirk my race, I am equally frustrated by my gender-defined role. I am a woman and thus to some extent expected to cook and have children and take orders—particularly in the field of house-construction. It's not the first time I've been aware of my gender putting me out of my "rightful" place, and I am as indignant about it here as I am at home.

I ask the man beside me what he is doing. He informs me that he is a carpenter and his work is done. I ask if he knows how to shovel and remind him that all of us have work until the building is done. He repeats his job title and reminds me that I am wrong.

I grab a shovel. With false self-confidence, I walk over to a mound of dirt and start flattening it. I am undermining the foreman and being culturally insensitive. I have no plan for what happens if the foreman laughs me away, or worse, gets angry.

I try to conceal the deep breaths I am taking to sustain my shoveling from the carpenter and the four other workers. I wonder if it is as obvious to these men how much I need their help; and in that need, how powerless I am.

With a purposeful stare and half an ironic smile I swallow and point out, "Well, I'm a teacher (the last job I had before coming to Liberia), and I know how to shovel." I try to look defiant and cute at the same time.

No one moves. They look at me, and I look at them. The breeze blows my hair gently into my face and I feel a critical mass of sweat begin to trickle from my ear down my neck, to the detriment of my defiance and cuteness. The foreman, forgotten paintbrush held vertically in one hand, allows paint to drip down his arm and his jaw to linger open. At least he doesn't seem angry.

Still no one moves. I turn back to the dirt pile and keep shoveling to buy time while I think. Just then school lets out across the street. One hundred children in white and blue uniforms pour out of the darkened rooms. It only takes one of them saying "Look-ah-de why-womah" ("Look at the white woman") before a small crowd forms.

I keep shoveling. With spectators, I even begin to shovel faster. I have long since stopped being able to conceal how out of breath I am. Women who sell small goods by the side of the road join the children. Young men on bikes park them and watch from the street. Teachers emerge from the schoolhouse to join them.

The carpenter moves toward me. I stop, in part because I will slow if I do not, and slowing is defeat. He puts out his hand, closing his eyes as he gives a quick upward nod. He is either impressed, shamed, or empathetic. I am too grateful to care. I hand off my implement. He effortlessly continues my labor.

My chest heaves as I turn to the next worker before the crowd dissipates to less than a critical mass. "Can you carry blocks?" I inquire as I pick up the left over concrete. Still shoveling, the carpenter yells over his shoulder, "Hey de hah-wohkey why woma-o." ("Help the hard working white woman.") Two others, both of whom had previously declared they were going to town, and were through working for today, step over to pick up more concrete. A third takes the wheelbarrow full of dirt to empty it in a ditch that needs filling.

"I can paint," I tell the foreman, holding out my hand. Paint still drips on his hand as he has not moved from the position in which I'd left him to shovel. He laughs—same laugh—and shakes his head. "Hah-wohkey why woma-o," he says as he hands me a brush and paint can. The real painter and I start on the front porch.

Work continues, each of us doing either his job or someone else's, until the contractor arrives to hand over the building. I buy lunch for all the workers. We walk down the hill to where they stay. Building materials cover the floor.

The contractor takes a share of meat and rice for himself and his friends to the table on the front porch, the only furniture in the house. He sends the workers to eat out of a communal bucket on the back steps. I decline an invitation to sit with the other high-rankers and instead go to the back step. We haven't learned each other's names, so I am still calling each by their skill, "carpenter," "painter" and they are still calling me "hah wokey why woma-o." Nonetheless, I feel camaraderie borne from our powerlessness and the appreciation that follows its relief.

Eating together on the back porch

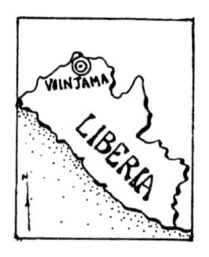

The Commander's Story

July 6, 2005
Voinjama, Liberia,
The Pakistani Battalion

The Pakistani Commander is plump and cheery with dark circles under his eyes, small baby teeth, tight thin lips, dimpled cheeks and a shy, wholesome laugh. His hair waves like lasagna pasta with a stark part neatly above his left eye. It is tamed from what must naturally expand to a notable helmet of curls. My colleague and I share lunch and dinner with the Commander each day in the officers' section of the mess hall while I am undertaking my latest task of testing a new set of voter and civic education materials on a northern Liberian audience.

On my second lunch with the Commander, I stay alone for tea. The hall empties as the officers retreat to their rooms to allow the dahl and rice to settle in privacy. From the corner the BBC is announcing that the 2012 Olympics will be held in London. There is confetti and cheering in the background as we discuss the international community and its responsibility, as a means of discussing our own responsibility.

The Commander plans to build roads, secure polling stations, and to offer help beyond his official UN mandate. "Liberia deserves the best we can offer," he tells me. I hear this periodically, but not all that often. But God, he sounds sincere.

For my part, I have been scrambling to meet my self-mandated challenge to repay in compliments the attentiveness he has required of all his officers on our behalf. I am using his conviction to insert yet another enthusiastic affirmation of his magnanimity. "I think I have not ever had such a strong and positive conversation about this." I wonder if I am telling the truth. In absence of accurate memory, I continue conscience free.

"I am so grateful that a person in your position feels that way. I keep thinking what an opportunity we all have, not only to have our own convictions, but to have the resources of institutions and the blessing of a mandate to do good." I have stroked his ego three-fold: the magnitude of his position, his person, and his institution. He is smiling largely and nodding. I am encouraged by his reassuring body language, "The last time I was here I spoke with your officers, and they commented that this was the best assignment of their lives because, as soldiers, it is not often that they are able to contribute to rebuilding. Isn't that lovely?" It is not just my words, it is my wide eyes, it is my forward lean, and my subservient stature—all efforts to be compelling. I am pleased with myself. I am a reasonably practiced complimenter, and I am on a roll. I want him to be pleased with himself as he has been unquestionably kind, but as is the way of complimenting—even for the reasonably practiced—the risk of evoking an unexpected response remains ever present.

It is not just that I want to thank him. I am mesmerized by the possibility of goodness, of greatness. I see sparks and flashes of an even better future. Within my soliloquy, the possibility smolders and grows, and I think, "What if this man's potential greatness is but one reminder away from combusting and exploding into reality?" With this genuine, if misleading, motive driving me ever forward, I continue.

"I can only imagine how grateful they must be for your conscientious leadership to enable their work to carry on seamlessly."

My words are thick with earnestness, which is all that saves them from sounding fake. I am not lying. I am impassioned and possibly blinded by my own struggle to see "goodness" triumph, and, despite my earlier self-reflections, I am not blowing smoke up anyone's nether regions.

The commander has not stopped smiling, but his eyes have glossed. His smile seems the remains of when he was listening, rather than an affirmation of his current agreement. His eyes begin to redden and wet.

"Isn't that a nice thing for them to have focused on?" I say, to fill the vacuum where a response would normally lie. I have not realized he is tearing up until the wet of his eyes seeps into the crevices below and begins to trace the edge of the dark circles.

I do not know what is culturally appropriate, professionally appropriate, or personally appropriate. I have known this man, this Commander, for two days—his officers snapping to attention, his presence quite suitably commanding. I sip my tea and dip my face into my cup farther than necessary to block him from my vision and offer a semblance of privacy. There is a long silence and I fake another sip of tea.

When the Commander breaks the silence, he tells me a story:

"On June 30th I had to go to a briefing in Monrovia—400 kilometers for a four-hour meeting. I was very annoyed, and then, for reasons, I missed my helicopter. Now I had to drive 400 kilometers for a four-hour meeting. I was so very annoyed."

"We set out in caravan and were driving for some time when we came upon a truck parked in the middle of the road—the middle of the road—so that no one could pass. All of us got out of our cars. I was furious at the irresponsibility, furious as I got out of the car, furious as I walked towards the truck, big yellow front looking at me, keeping me from passing."

Two aid trucks stuck in mud on the Voinjama road

He makes angry faces at his own hand, which he holds up in front of his face to demonstrate the yellow truck mocking his efforts to pass.

"We were all, all of us, yelling, but I was the first yelling, the first to walk around the truck with the big yellow front. No one else saw them. There were ten of them, or more. They had been stuck for some time. There was no food left. They spoke almost no English. And so I did not understand their pleading, and they could not, for the most part, understand my yelling. I heard the bits and pieces and they heard the tone. I was still furious. And then . . ."

He pauses again. He is peering at me as if the story is happening somewhere in the back of my head and he can see it if he looks closely.

"And then a woman came to me with her child and she pulled open her shirt. Still looking at my eyes, she showed her breast, held up her child, and with the hand that had just ripped open her clothing, she made a motion of a flat line and said, 'Nothing.' There was no question about what she was telling me. But still I was furious."

He is looking directly into my eyes without making eye contact.

"Still I was furious. And I turned from her and began to walk away. Still furious. Before I rounded the truck I heard the woman begin to cry. Low. Desperate. And only then did my fury quiet, and I realized how much fear was around me in the starving people who had been sleeping behind the truck. It was so easy to be part of that fear, to walk away furious. It is not so difficult to be the hope."

And for the first time since his story started, I sense that I am again an integral part of the conversation.

"And as I heard the mother cry, I felt a powerful desire to be part of the hope. I never went to the conference. For the next two days, I drove each of those people to their intended destinations. They had only brought enough food for two days and they'd been stuck for six when I met them, and so I fed them as well. Finally I was part of the hope."

His story finished and I nodded in empathy, but not in clarity. I had spoken of his officers, then of him. He had glazed, remembered this story, then cried. That the memory of the experience caused the tears is clear, but still, I am not sure if his story was a catharsis for hypocrisy, brought on by my inappropriately lavish compliments, or if he was crying for the desperation of the country (completely self-unaware), or if the depth of his personal growth brought him to tears.

As murky to me as what his story meant to him, is what our story means to me. That I am affected is clear, but still I am not sure what my lesson is. Is it about me, a caution to temper my impulse to sincere but misdirected flattery? Is it about him, the responsibility and the hope? Is it about Liberia and its desperation for someone to understand and respond with humanity? Perhaps it is about us: about the ability of a person to affect and be affected by others.

We Are What We've Been

August 12, 2005
Monrovia, Liberia

In Liberia it's smacking me in the face more than any travel I've done before. I am small town southern. I feel it in my bones, my smile, my flirtation, the way I walk through a door, the way I listen, the way I accept or don't accept drinks, the way I approach election assistance, and in my political analysis. I understand economic depression as a southerner. I know chips-on-shoulders as a southerner. I've given my phone number out to half of Monrovia and wave to the other half like I know them because I'm from po-dunk Virginia. I am not claiming that these things are all exclusively southern, but rather that my approach is stereotypically so. It shocks me how little I deviate from that which produced me. I am such a reflection of the generations before me that my very existence challenges the notion of free will.

It started as a self-realization but is steadily morphing into a sense that Liberians are similarly bound. We each will the world to conform to our determination of what already is.

For one Liberian I speak to after another, this instinct to explain the present as a reiteration of the past is a manifestation of a profound sense of their nation's desperation, its inability to function, and its worthlessness. For them, life happens across a backdrop of tragedy and depressing truths.

Liberians' damning self-descriptions have only become more frequent as the campaign period approaches. Despite the encouraging experiences of registration and exhibition, many Liberians worry that campaigning will be just as the country has been for decades before: fraught with violent outbreaks. Fourteen-year-old Liberians have never known peace. Thirty-year-old Liberians have just now lived a greater percentage of their lives out of war than during it. And the post-conflict peace

The Bopolu police department

is a tenuous one, where the fittest fill their coffers while the internationals will still bring in the cash to go around. When the gravy train of the election sets off and international aid and peacekeepers leave, what then?

When there is corruption in government, Liberia turns, humiliated once again, to the international community and says, "We are not built as you are, we are corrupt people," instead of raging, "our senators are paid forty dollars a month, our civil servants have not been paid for half of a year. Until we fix our damaged system, we will always spend more fighting the corruption of those expected to live on impossibly low salaries, than accomplishing anything for the country."

Where Liberians fall short in entitlement, I fill in the gap. I'm an American, nothing if not entitled. "You deserve better," I inform them. It's a heartless badgering, as I know there are countless hurdles to overcome. I know an election does not a democracy guarantee, a democracy does not ensure development, and development will never be justly dispersed. I want to tell them their future will be different than their past, but I come from a place where two hundred years after our civil war we still hear the claim, "The South Will Rise Again." I am a Southerner. Who am I to say, "forget the past?"

It's Time

September 11, 2005
Monrovia, Liberia
My House

I have to return home, to where I make sense to myself, to where the world makes more sense to me. I'm leaving Liberia a month before the elections, which is shocking to most of my friends, but I have gone past my ability to function. I'm tired. I don't remember why I'm here.

Junior was a curmudgeonly homeless man who called me his "mama." I was never sure if it was a ploy for money, but I'd taken to him months before, when I had found out he had a daughter with an HIV positive woman who could not breast feed. I had helped him through countless illnesses and cans of formula since then and enjoyed daily updates in varying degrees of grumpiness on my way in and out of work.

He was always trying to convince me to get him 'African medicine.' I was forever declining and sending him to the free MSF clinic next to my house. On Monday, I'd found him collapsed outside my office door, sweaty, stinking, tears streaming from his desperate eyes. "Mama, I need African medicine."

"I'm getting you an ambulance," I tell him as I pull out my cell phone.

He grabs my arm, and I look down at the grime in his fingernails and the softness in his resign, "Don't leave me, I'm dying, mama."

The ex-combatants outside my office

His skin is hot and his stomach distended. I squat and curl up next to him on the sidewalk leaning against a pile of rocks that has been there for months, and was originally intended to fill the potholes the street. "I'm not leaving you, we're getting you to a doctor." He looks at me silently and, without words, he pleads for me take him to a medicine man. But I will not relent. I am going to fix it my way, damn it. I have the best technology in the world behind me.

I've been told there are only four working ambulances for the public in the country. This may be an exaggeration, but it's still almost impossible to get through on an emergency line—a line which is, by virtue of its telephone-ness, only accessible to the wealthier individuals with cell phones (landlines haven't functioned for years). I try 911 more than 30 times in a row, hanging up and redialing with each busy signal, as Junior trembles beside me. A crowd of helpless onlookers forms around us blocking the sidewalk even further. Time is passing, Junior is too ill to be visibly worsening and in too much pain even to beg for more or different help.

I tell Junior I'll be back. I pause to make sure he's seen my resolve before darting to my office, leaping up steps three at a time. They stop a staff meeting to call all our NGO friends and finally, as something of a personal favor to one of my colleagues, musters an ambulance to take him to MSF.

That was the last time I saw him alive. I know that he arrived at the hospital, was given medication, and checked himself out. I imagine he had once again, and for the last time, not taken his 'western medicine,' gone in search of a local remedy and, once again, and for the last time, been denied any remedy at all through our inability to come to an agreement. It occurs to me that no amount of technology will cure someone unless you listen to what treatment they are willing to accept.

Five ex-combatants who begged with him hurry over to me on crutches and in their wheel chairs, "We are sorry, missy, your son has died." They mimic the useless way his hands curved in as they tell me, in case I am not sure which son they mean, I suppose. They take up a collection for his burial. There is a viewing in the slum on the beach. If I want, they will take me. I imagine him curled on the beach as he had been curled with me on the pile of rocks. He is child-like, vulnerable, and dead. I lose it, start crying, and cannot go. The ex-combatants comfort me with their remaining limbs.

The next day is Rita's birthday and we have a party. While we sit around eating cake I learn of how Barcon's son was killed during the war; how my driver was shot, along with five of his best friends, and only he survived. I learn from one of my security guards that, while at gunpoint, he'd held down a man as someone else macheted his head off. Maybe it's because I'm mixing these stories with my own from September 11, 2001, or maybe not—these lives and lives lost stand on their own, certainly—but I've started to see death and desperation everywhere and I no longer know how to bear it.

Fireflies and Fullfillment

September 20, 2005
Lexington, Virginia
My Back Porch

Fireflies climb slowly out of the grass at dusk and rise into the trees as the sun sinks and the sky purples and blackens. This nocturnal light ballet is a source of family pride and offers tranquility. My father brings me a fruit smoothie, his specialty. He adds mango. I understand he has added mango because they have mangoes in Africa. I smile and am grateful. My dad is a retired professor and now has more time on his hands than he is accustomed to having. And so, while my mom frantically opens the world to 110 high-school history students, we run errands together and sit quietly in each other's presence. I don't know what we say about Liberia. I don't know if we say anything. I think I may have talked about it a lot, but I also might not have said anything at all. Being home has acquired the same dreamlike quality of old memories and independent movies.

At night I have nightmares of terrible things, death camps and mass slaughters. I'm either one step ahead of my demise or negotiating freedom for my helpless companions with some careless, evil giant. I have a particularly upsetting recurring dream in which I am allowing people to die, and it's worse than impotency, it's disregard.

When I wake up in the morning, these images linger, but they mix with others too. I keep safe and constant the image of

Rita with her voter's card, able to choose her country's leader for the first time in her life. And her vote counts equally with all the warlords, and teachers who "know book," and more than Charles Taylor and the Lebanese family who took her away, because they can't vote. And it's beautiful, and it's right. And I'm part of making that happen. And I cannot defend my faith in the goodness of this, but my doubt and cynicism mute, and I can feel again that my work in Liberia matters. Even if I'm kidding myself about what I can do to ease the pain of the civil war, or what democracy will do to assist the transition to peace, what I have done matters. I get it together; I fight off my exhaustion and extend my contract. Two weeks after leaving, I return to Liberia.

Children at a wedding in Monrovia

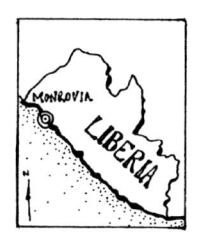

I'm Back

September 23, 2005
Monrovia, Liberia
My House

I am back in my bed, in my room next to the medieval village. I can hear my roommate ambling about, opening and closing his squeaky door, puttering into and out of the bathroom. The loud buzz of the fan doesn't quite drown out the thunder. But neither does the generator entirely obscure the sound of the crashing waves. Curtains mottled yellow and brown sway softly in the sticky breeze, and the fragrance of hot bodies and burning wood wafts about me in varying degrees of detectability. Taped to my house, door, mirror, and bed are a series of welcomes and well-wishings that Rita and Barcon commissioned the guards to write for my arrival.

I have returned with fewer illusions of grandeur. I did not board the plane intending to be part of the nucleus. I'm not even sure exactly why I've returned, but I had to. In the same way I had to leave, I had to come back.

Looking over at my neighbors across the razor wire, I remember how much I wanted them to "show up" for the registration. I wanted them to believe in my work, to believe in Democracy, and now that I am back, I have lost certainty in my cause. I'm still riddled with these depressing questions and, even more detrimentally, afraid of getting wrapped up in the same way as Liberia is wrapped up in "the election." We'll just make it work, and then it will all be ok—decades of civil war erased by a paper ballot and a choice. When it's done will we say cliché things like, "now the real work starts?" And then leave?

I fear all of this, but, while I have lost certainty, I have not lost faith... When I fall asleep tonight, I will imagine Rita on the day of the election, empowered and beautiful, making her own choice, and maybe I'll leave thinking there is a chance. I want to leave on those terms, even if it is an illusion. I have at least moved through the spectrum of detachment. I am committed to giving Liberia all the good I have until I leave. If I do that, I will have treated this as home, and I cannot do better.

A sunset off Monrovia

The Election Commeth

October 9, 2005
Monrovia, Liberia
My Hotel Room

I have set up shop and sick-room in a bright, moldy room in the Mamba Point Hotel, the same hotel in which I spent much of my first and second months in-country. In this way I have managed to come full circle, but the remainder of my experience has not had the resolution that symmetry provides, and for that I am agitated.

The election of Liberia's new President, Vice-President, Senate, and House of Representatives is two days away, and for the last seven months I have worked thousands of hours with thousands of others trying to make good on international promises for a fair, transparent, and (most important to me) useful election. Since my arrival in April, I have been part of a countrywide obsession with these elections. This country breathes with the election calendar and pulses with its promises in a way that my own does not—or at least has not in my lifetime.

Last week, however, I was diagnosed with malaria and typhoid and have been quarantined ever since. In the past six days, I've held down only three meals, but two of those were in the last 24 hours. I've also stopped sweating through my clothes, which gives me reason to believe I'm improving. If I don't pass medical clearance tomorrow, I'll spend October 11th watching what I have come to think of as the "birth of my child" on satellite news broadcasts in a three-minute insert within the twenty-four hour coverage of the South Asia Earthquake and Hurricane Stan in Guatemala.

Jimmy Carter is here to observe the elections and is holding a press conference in the hotel. The jovial banter of his Secret Service personnel on the balcony outside my room punctuates the swish and chatter of the evening rain. It sounds like a school field trip out there—hotel doors opening and closing, the patter of excited footsteps, animated greetings, late night laughing, and that American accent.

Voters waiting in line on election day

Election Day

October 11, 2005
Monrovia, Liberia
My Hotel Room

I did not pass medical clearance. I beg a friend to take me out anyway. He packs me into his car and we drive around Monrovia for an hour until I tire. Lines are outrageously long and docile. I'm giddy, but then my head starts to pound out of my ears, and I retreat to the darkness of my room again. I have a network of observers and colleagues sending me text updates from around the country. Everywhere the same story, long obedient lines, a few minor incidents resulting from too many people, too few polling stations. Given so many people's fears, there is a shocking absence of violence.

Five peacekeepers died this week, but they were on leave at home in Kashmir, killed by the earthquake I have been following so closely on satellite news. I write a letter to the Pakistani Commander. I have been told that one hundred and fifty family members of the men in his battalion were also killed in the earthquake. Someone from the UN is traveling north this week and is taking our letters of condolence. Despite the losses, the battalion deployed today, all over the north in areas where rebels once held ground. Observers and friends confirm peace across the region.

Rita comes by with her inked finger and voter's card. We talk about her boyfriend, who seems to be acting like his usual ornery self. My former colleagues from The Carter Center bring fruit. We talk about the opening of the new grocery store, which imports things like peaches. The maid brings up flowers. We talk about how the rainy season is finally coming to an end and now we'll have the new season with all its new vegetation. Life, normal life, is happening, and it is happening because in many ways the election is actually a non-event. No violence, no struggle. Even the weather has cooperated.

Tomorrow, outside and down the colorful, sooty street, there will be noise, and dust, and potholes, and miniature business ventures, and progress, and the rock and gurgle of life will continue. The rhythms of Monrovia will still be marked at once by nation-wide and decades-long unpredictability, as well as the inertia of humanity's will to maintain, to continue. Over one block, just down from the Lebanese hairdressers, my former boss will,

A polling officer explains the voting process

no doubt, sit outside the office on the porch furniture, working without electricity as her generator once again succumbs to the elements. Something near 40% of the staff will come down with a non-descript tropical ailment. And around the corner, yet again, just right of Gyude Bryant's tank, the squatter's house and Frances' shabeen, Rita and Barcon will be making my house a home.

This election may be the beginning or the beginning of the end. I have not found a more convincing prediction for Liberia's future than I have for the ultimate effects of those infomercial dream diets. What I can say definitively about Liberia, or even about my Liberian experience, is limited.

I can say that my time in Liberia has taught me that no person, group, or country can overcome another country's problems and determine through sheer will what blessed future it will enjoy. Until we, the "Democracy Builders," the "Do-Gooders," the "International Community," the people who want to affect change, internalize this lesson, we will amass infrastructure without diminishing the problems. We may show up to the meetings, but regardless of our intentions, we will miss being part of the hope. We will live to sweat it out another day, but if we do not understand the needs of those for whom we work; if we do not understand Rita's need to "know book," or Junior's desire for African medicine, then we will fail.

"It All"

October 16, 2005
Monrovia, Liberia
Robertsfield International Airport

I've lost ten pounds in the last week and a half. The persistence of inexplicable nausea, neck pain, stomachaches, fever, and loss of appetite have sent me back to the clinic for another full run of tests. Not much to show for it. Low white blood cell count, but that is about it. Now I am being medically evacuated to somewhere they can run more than typhoid and malaria tests. I am being sent back to the U.S.

I will step on the plane with images of fireflies, and smoothies, bluegrass music, the sweet smell of wet lawn and dry leaves. But as I show my passport and confirm my vegetarian meal, I will hear Barcon's barrel voice and Rita's laugh with the ocean in the back ground, I'll hear myself saying, "You tell me what you want to accomplish in this country. We can do it, you know. We are given that privilege." I'll see little Nealin opening her eyes and the foreman's splatter-painted hands; and I'll feel the wind through the portal of the helicopter window, the ocean of broccoli trees below, and the gutted tears of the commander; and I'll smell that Liberian smell of burnt wood and sweaty bodies.

I am leaving Liberia again and I will have to continue the quest for my place, myself, and "It All" in some other location. But I am home. Neither in Liberia nor out of Liberia. I am home because "It All" does not happen in a geographic location, nor is "It All" an event. "It All" was not the election, but what the election helped make possible, just normal life.

The End

Nealin and Rita, Thinker's Village
(Photograph by Ashley Barr)

Also from the Crumpled Press

13 Poems
by Jordan McIntyre
Poetry

When I Wished I Was Here:
Dispatches From Fallujah
by Derek McGee
Non-Fiction

What's On, What's Coming Off?
by Mario Bick
Cultural Theory

Malarian Frutarian
by Robert Albert
Memoir

911
by Nicholas Jahr
Fiction

About the Authors

J. Nealin Parker, a former elections consultant in Liberia, has traveled in almost 40 countries and hopes, one day, to truly understand even one of them. Her photographs and writing have previously appeared in the *Lexington News Gazette*. She is currently pursuing a Masters degree at Princeton University's Woodrow Wilson School of Public and International Affairs.

Ambassador Jacques Paul Klein served as Special Representative of the Secretary General and Coordinator of UN Operations in Liberia from 2003-2005. He previously served as Special Representative and Coordinator of UN Operations in Bosnia-Herzegovina. A retired Major-General in the U.S. Air Force, Ambassador Klein is a career member of the Senior U.S. Foreign Service and a member of the Council on Foreign Relations.

Colophon

This limited edition book was designed by Jordan McIntyre and Alexander Bick in close consultation with the author. The text was laser-printed in *Adobe Garamond Pro* at 10.5/13.5 on 80 lb. Mohawk Superfine text paper in an eggshell finish. The cover and endpapers are 360 gram Fabriano Murillo in grey and India Batik Solids in periwinkle. The outer jacket and color plates were produced by the Manahawkin Printing Company.

Except where otherwise noted,
all photographs and drawings
are by J. Nealin Parker.

Hand-bound in Cranbury, New Jersey

by ~~JNM~~ as number **1 4 1**